Awaken the Supernatural You!

By Robert Rite

Table of Contents:

Chapter 1 - There is a Little Supernatural in all of us!

Mankind has an innate need and desire to experience the supernatural realm. We know that there is more out there than we can we can see, hear, touch, taste, and smell. Although we do not see it, we can all sense that there exists a supernatural power that controls the movement of the stars, the wind, life and death. Many of us at times feel frustrated and so powerless when we contemplate the enormity of our universe, and how apparently disconnected we are from the other dimension(s) outside of ours. The good news is that our creator intentionally developed this innate need in our psyche because he wants us to seek him out. And when we find him, we can indeed experience divine supernatural power.

Nobody shares your DNA, fingerprint, eyes, voice, walk, face, smile, personality, character or mind - you are 100% unique! There never has been and there will never be another you! That is what God thinks of you and how much he loves you! You are special - you are one of a kind before the throne of God Almighty. Indeed, we are all different, and we all can make a difference in this earth in a unique manner that no one else can. God designed you for a specific purpose on this side of the heavens.

To seek out the mysteries of heaven is to nurture our spiritual growth and to become more useful to God - otherwise we are never going to mature to our fullest. We can't just live in the now - we need to live in the supernatural.

God is the master of creativity - and he alone created everything. His level of creativity is endless. Since we are created in his own image there is no doubt that each of us has a unique creative spirit. When we release this spiritual power and apply our unique gifts towards "something", nobody can create that "something" that God wants us to create better than we can!

When you consider the magic behind computers, smart phones, tablets, space travel and all of the modern age products and gadgets that we enjoy today, you have to admit that there must exist some kind of supernatural element behind all of these man-made creations. As we consider further, we can only conclude that our supernatural brain allows us to create supernatural like systems and things.

Upon reading this book I hope that you will come to understand that there is indeed Supernatural power in all of us, and that we are not limited to just creating within the confines of this natural world. When we understand the potential that our creator imparted upon each of us, we will realize that it is quite natural to be supernatural!

Do you think that some of the multi-billionaires out there received their great wealth through their own hard work? Well of course not because their minds were created by the same God who created ours. God enables the mind and releases energy and ideas that can create supernatural-like innovations for the betterment and enjoyment of all mankind.

These fellow "pioneers" merely took action on whatever idea or gift they received from God. They became aware of their particular gifts and talents, and then employed much creative energy to develop or improve on something that fulfilled a need that most people or companies needed or wanted. As a result they became very wealthy.

Who these super wealthy credit and what they do with that wealth will be the test of their spiritual fabric. Hopefully they will have enough wisdom to give the credit to God...the source of all ideas, talents, riches and blessings. But as rich as these folks become, they don't come close to the wealth that Solomon had because God blessed him with wealth and wisdom beyond any other man because his priorities and heart were in the right place (1 Kings 9-14). Let's set our priorities and heart in the right place as well, because when God blesses it surpasses anything that man can accomplish on his or her own. God's limits are boundless.

Just like these billionaire folks, when our priorities and faith are in the right place, our potential is unlimited while here on earth. But the measure of true success is whether what we achieve while here on earth is in accordance with God's plan for us. When our time is up, anything else will stay behind - along with whatever wealth we acquired on earth. Yes, even the wisest and richest man to ever walk the earth was not content with the enormous wealth he had accumulated. King Solomon alluded to this when he concluded: "...*I hated all the things I had labored for under the sun, because I must leave them to the one who comes after me. And who knows whether that person will be wise or foolish? Yet they will have control over all the fruit of my labor into which I have poured my effort and skill under the sun...*" (Ecclesiastes 2:17-19)."

No doubt that it must be wonderful to experience the life of the super rich. But no amount of wealth accumulated here on earth compares to the abundance of joy and peace that we will enjoy in paradise.

No matter what others may have told you in the past or present, your potential is unlimited. In those moments when you feel lonely, abandoned and unloved, just look up and allow your heavenly father to shower you with the supernatural love that he offers you.

God gave mankind free will to rule this planet as we saw fit (Mathew 16:19; 18:18). This is why history in this planet is pretty much written by mankind. History shapes itself based on our unified actions. The history books are written by mankind under certain parameters and limitations that God has imposed upon us - for our own good!

God loved us so much that he gave us total dominion over planet earth. Satan deceived Adam out of that inheritance. But when Jesus died at the cross he restored that dominion back into our hands. As a result, we can once again rule over demons, illness, alcohol and drug addiction, poverty, and any other affliction that hinders the quality of our life.

God wants us and allows us to fulfill our hearts desires (Psalm 37:4). But it is up to us to choose desires that are in line with God's character. When we choose desires that are ungodly, then we may open ourselves to trials, perhaps trials that jeopardize our life or that lead to lifetime consequences.

God provides us with a lot of space so that we can mature in the spirit, and achieve our maximum potential with every one of the gifts and talents that he has imparted upon us. He takes great pleasure in observing us maximizing our potential, and when we reach one milestone God blesses us with even more potential. In John 10:10 Jesus says "....*I **have** come that they may **have life**, and **have** it abundantly.*"

God values his creation since he made you and me in his very own image. Jesus calls his saved children his friends even though he is our Lord and savior. He does not want us to be just a servant! We are his friends because we know what he wants for us and we know what he needs from us, In John 15:15 we read *"I no longer call you* servants, because a servant does not know his master's business. Instead, I have called you friends, for everything that I learned from my Father I have made known to you."

You see, God wants each of us to have an intimate relationship with him. He loves that we serve him, but we are much more to him than just a servant. A father and son that have a great relationship really do feel like best friends and have very confident and open conversations. There is nothing the father would not do for the son and vice versa (John 15:7). This is what an intimate relationship is really all about, and this is what God would like to have with each of us.

Upon Christ's death at the cross we inherited supernatural power to carry on the good works that Jesus demonstrated during his short life. 1 Cor. 3:21-23, Deuteronomy 29:29). This inheritance is ours to put to work in the here and now. It is not meant to be unopened baggage that we take with us to heaven, and open it there! There is already an abundance of kingdom power there - they don't need anymore! Kingdom power is meant to be used up in the present, not in the future. The harvest is waiting to be gathered up for God (John 4:35)

Despite the title, this book has nothing to do with the occult belief of obtaining power from unknown dark forces. When one obtains power from dark forces, that dangerous practice always leads to confusion, disappointments and tragedy in one's life. This book is about acquiring supernatural results from the correct source.

In these troubled times it is so easy to be swayed and to lose focus on or abandon God altogether unless we are equipped with the truth. In this book we discuss the only ways to release supernatural power and blessings into our life without any dangerous occult practices and the consequences thereof.

We are not merely human beings! When we accept the Holy Spirit and allow it to fully influence our mind and our life, we can live and operate with supernatural power.

Chapter 2 - Getting Our Priorities Strait

It is good to set goals for ourselves in many areas of our life. These can include education, career, financial, marriage, family and spiritual goals - the later being the most important.

When I was young, having my own business someday and being financially secure was a major goal for me. There is nothing wrong with that goal, but when it becomes an obsession and it preoccupies your mind 24/7 you have in essence made materialism your idol; you're God. Greed and any preoccupation with the pleasures of this world always lead us in the wrong path.

For each of us our lifelong goal should be to have an intimate relationship with our creator, and to do our part in establishing God's kingdom here on earth. Ask God to lead your thoughts and direct your path. With God on your side you can achieve anything in life that you want, and whatever you achieve through God always lasts a lifetime - and beyond! The pleasures of the flesh and the things of this world are temporary, and are irrelevant over time. All the Carnal distractions of life are "chasing after wind" as Solomon put it in the book of Ecclesiastes.

The true church is not a physical church. We collectively are the church, and the kingdom of God operates through each one of us. When this kingdom of God is manifested through us we create a **heaven-on-earth** phenomenon where the sick are healed, limbs are restored, families are reunited, and all types of miracles take place.

Some have been misled into thinking that a life under God means that we are reduced to a boring life void of "fun". They fail to believe Jesus promise that a life under God is a life full of abundance **John 10:10**. We are not talking about just an abundance of love, but of whatever we ask that is in line with God's best plans for our life - this includes blessings in our job, finances, health, mindset, and for our family, children, and grandchildren. When God blesses - it is the real thing. These are blessings that not only benefit you but your entire family. When God promises abundance - he means abundance. God never breaks promises because unlike us - he is perfect.

But God will never invade your space - He does not need to beg. He places great respect upon our will. He wants us to choose whether we want him in our life or not. How sad that many have chosen to keep God out of their lives. And yet God allows many of them to live apparently blessed and fulfilling lives even when they choose to go it alone.

Unfortunately these folks will live their entire life being more vulnerable to all types of tragedies and attacks from the evil one, void of the protection blessings and fullness that God wants them to enjoy. They will never know how much more productive and blessed their life could have been with God at its center, guiding their every step. It is a testament of God's great mercy that many unsaved souls still make it through life unscathed.

It is important to understand that the purpose of receiving spiritual blessings in our life is not just so that we can live an abundant life full of joy and fulfillment, but also to expand God's kingdom here on earth.

Ask God and Jesus to come into your life. You want to develop an intimate love relationship with the lord because that is the way we can feel and explain the depth of God's love and power.

The gift of the Holy Spirit was provided so that we could overcome the flesh, temptations, tormenting, diseases and all of the other afflictions from Satan.

Jesus told us that he is the vine and we are his branches, if his word abides in us than we can ask whatever we desire and it will be done (John 15:7). We are an integral part of his and just like branches spread out, we are to spread the works of the Lord among our fellow man. **Read also John 14:17 and John 17:21; 1 Corinthians 12:12**.

Chapter 3 - Love and faith - the Magic Formula

Ephesians 3:18-19, Romans 5:5 all explain how love is instrumental in releasing kingdom power.

All creation, blessings and life itself emanates from God's love. Healing, health, joy, happiness, all flow from God's love. Love is what God blesses us with - it is our anointing, our blessing, and our grace.

Love is the anointing for healing, prospering, deliverance, peace and removal of all burdens and yokes. None of this can operate in our lives outside of the circle of Love.

Faith is alive when there is Love. Fear, doubt and selfishness (and all sin) operates in the absence of Love. Faith operates in the presence of Love. Fear is unbelief because there is no fear in love.

Spiritual love is a reflection of God's spirit. It is God's love manifested in you by the gift of the Holy Spirit. This is an unconditional (agape) love. Emotional love on the other hand is conditional, i.e. I will love you **IF** you do this or that first. It is kind of an artificial type of love - a love of convenience.

You cannot love your enemy as Jesus commanded with just emotional love. Only Jesus supernatural agape love can allow us to love our enemies. It is imparted to us though the gift of the Holy Spirit.

What is love? "Love is patient, love is kind. It does not envy, it does not boast, it is not proud. It does not dishonor others, it is not self-seeking, it is not easily angered, and it keeps no record of wrongs. Love does not delight in evil but rejoices with the truth. It always protects, always trusts, always hopes, and always perseveres. Love never fails." (**1 Corinthians 13:4-8**)

Contemporary media (music, TV, Movies) and the world, whether satanically inspired or not, inspire us to shun away from Christian values and to embrace worldly values and its physical desires. Not the spiritual desires of our soul. Everything the media relishes are external; and relishes nothing that is God inspired.

Faith works by love and fear by selfishness. Love is the power that permits God to perform great blessings in our lives. Without the love of God, we won't see the power that love offers for our lives. Love casts out fear because love does not want us to be tormented by fear. **1 John 4:18** "There is no fear in love. But perfect love drives out fear, because fear has to do with punishment. The one who fears is not made perfect in love."

Perfect Love is the Christian who keeps God's word. Fear, hatred, and stress are flushed out when love is perfected.

God does indeed recognize and reward our love. For example, King Solomon loved the Lord so much that he once sacrificed 1000 burnt offerings to the Lord. That very night God appeared to him in a dream and asked him "what can I do for you". Read 2 Chronicles 1:6-12

Doing anything without love will not profit you: 1 Corinthians 13:3 also see: 2 Corinthians 9:7 each of you should give what you have decided in your heart to give, not reluctantly or under compulsion, for God loves a cheerful giver.

Now the devil knows that God is love. So he will endeavor to keep us out of love by bombarding us with all of the problems and challenges that life brings - anything that can turn our love to anger, and hatred. This includes all of the daily issues we are confronted with, such as annoying people, insults, traffic jams, disappointments, marital issues, being offended, feeling hurt, a horrible boss, disrespect, fear, etc.

Fear is a tool that evil uses to fulfill his mission of putting us in a place of unbelief and to thus eliminate or reduce our blessings. The seed of fear contradicts God's word and his promises for our lives. So that is why we need to read and know God's word. Read: **2 Timothy 1:6-7** 6 For this reason I remind you to fan into flame **the gift of God**, which is in you through the laying on of my hands. 7 For the Spirit God gave us does not make us timid, but **gives us power, and of love and of a sound mind**.

1 John 4:7 7 Dear friends, let us love one another, for love comes from God. Everyone who loves has been born of God and knows God. 8 *Whoever does not love does not know God, because God is love.*

1 John 5:1 1 everyone who believes that Jesus is the Christ is born of God and everyone who loves the father loves his child as well. 2 This is how we know that we love the children of God: by loving God and carrying out his commands. 3 In fact, this is love for God: to keep his commands. *And his commandments are not burdensome.*

1 John 2:5 5 but if anyone obeys his word, love for God is truly made complete in them.

Psalms 1:1-2 [1] Blessed is the one who does not walk in step with the wicked or stand in the way that sinners take or sit in the company of mockers, [2] *but whose delight is in the law of the LORD, and who meditates on his law day and night.* [3] That person is like a tree planted by streams of water, which yields its fruit in season and whose leaf does not wither—whatever they do prospers.

Psalms 112:1 Praise the LORD. Blessed are those who fear the LORD, who find great delight in his commands.

So when we are asked why you are a Christian, your answer should be because you love God. God is love, and if we do not love God how do we expect to make it to heaven?

Psalm 16:11 [11] you make known to me the path of life; you will fill me with joy in your presence, with eternal pleasures at your right hand.

1 Chronicles 29: [2] With all my resources I have provided for the temple of my God—gold for the gold work, silver for the silver, bronze for the bronze, iron for the iron and wood for the wood, as well as onyx for the settings, turquoise, stones of various colors, and all kinds of fine stone and marble—all of these in large quantities. [3] Besides, in my devotion to the temple of my God I now give my personal treasures of gold and silver for the temple of my God, over and above everything I have provided for this holy temple.

Psalm 37:4 Take delight in the LORD, and he will give you the desires of your heart. Matthew 6:33: But seek first his kingdom and his righteousness, and all these things will be given to you as well.

Love allows us to come into the presence of our Lord. Love causes Jesus to commit to manifestation in our lives, as we read in **John 14:21:** "Whoever has my commands and keeps them is the one who loves me. The one who loves me will be loved by my Father, **and I too will love them** and show myself to them."

Your faith can only operate through love (Galatians 5:6). Love is the crucial ingredient to activate faith. This is because God's character is love (1 Corinthians 13:1). The love of Christ is what we need in order to be able to perform the works that he performed in his time. It is available to all of us through the Holy Spirit. Love is what provides us with God's character of compassion, empathy, kindness, mercy, gentleness and all of the traits that enable us to heal ourselves and others and perform all kinds of miraculous works for the glory of the Lord.

Faith manifests kingdom power. Faith is the fuel that releases kingdom power through us. Without faith we cannot execute any power from God (Hebrews 11:6). We need to become saved in order to have the full measure of heavenly faith. This is a level of faith that releases power from heaven (John 3:1-8; mark 11:22).

Faith is the evidence of things not seen (Hebrews 11:1), and that is why it unleashes the power to make the impossible - possible when proved by revelation from the Holy Spirit. In other words faith sees into the invisible realm and makes what might appear as impossible to carnal man, possible to those who operate in the kingdom of God. Faith comes by hearing (by knowledge and revelation), and hearing by the word of God (Romans 10:17).

The source of divine knowledge is the bible. We must know as many versus from the bible as possible because we cannot apply Gods words in faith if we don't know them!

Many people suffer from the bondage of fear. They may fear rejection, heights, failure, public speaking, hospitals or whatever. Understand that fear is not from God, because fear is the opposite of faith and love. If someone attacks your child or a parent you will fearlessly defend them. Why? Because Love is the opposite of fear and love conquers fear! God is love!

Chapter 4 - The Fallen Church and the Lack of Miracles

God made us to live extraordinary lives in abundance, but unfortunately most churches today are preaching an incomplete or substitute form of Gospel that is void of healing, and miracles.

This is contrary to what the apostles demonstrated. All the apostles preached this message of the kingdom of God and the power thereof. Acts 2:14-41; 8:4-12, Romans 15:18-19, Hebrews 2:3-4. Mark 16:15-18; 16:20. Mathew 28:19. And this mandate still stands (read Mathew 10:7).

Since most churches no longer conduct healing masses or other demonstrations of faith it is getting harder to observe these miracles. Yet the gospel of the Kingdom is all about healing, miracles, saving and casting out demons. Faith without works is dead (James 2:20).

Throughout Christian history our ministers and leaders have failed to sear these truths into the minds of their youth and as a result revivals are too far and few between. So now we see in these later days' whole generations of adults and young adults searching for supernatural power, and spiritual knowledge in all the wrong places. Witchcraft, the occult, and new age thinking are the predominant religions of our society today. Satan has a stronghold on the majority because past generations of pastors and ministers failed to do their job. They were content with preaching to the choir, and preaching whatever made the choir "feel good". As a result this is now the normal in the vast number of houses of worship.

This ambivalence to the word of God has turned institutions such as Yale University from a pillar of supernatural revivalism that it originally was to just another one of many secular institutions that shuns the word of God. Society as a whole from the once great institutions, governments, public schools, the Supreme Court, the media and just about every other entity has yielded to Satan's influence. And people wonder why miracles and supernatural manifestations of God are so hard to witness. God is hungry for Holy Spirit filled warriors that can revive the world out of its spiritual coma, before it is too late.

A lot of people receive counseling at their church or elsewhere when in fact what they need is deliverance. There are millions (perhaps billions) of good people out there that are walking around with demons in their body and they are unaware of it. They need deliverance rather than pep talks. These demons may be the cause of their, anxiety, depression, arthritis, cancer, evil thoughts, unforgiveness, hatred, bitterness, selfishness, and just about any carnal weaknesses that we may have. Yes, our enemy hates us and wants to attack us anyway and in any manner that we allow him to or grant him access.

Satan wants us to fear supernatural phenomenon such as miracles because he does not want us to believe or partake in any healing of others or ourselves because he wants to keep us in bondage, and under his control. He wants people to feel uncomfortable with these manifestations as if they were a cult or strange sect, when it is exactly what the Messiah wants us to do on his behalf here on earth! 1 Corinthians 12:28.

Today many churches do not teach nor practice healing, the very thing that Jesus demonstrated and focused on during his 3 year ministry. The church leaders through the ages have decided to fall for the satanic belief that healing is from the devil! That is how deluded many churches have become. They have rejected the good news of the gospel. What Jesus so clearly taught and demonstrated - his own flock has swept under the rug. What a shame. It is for this reason that so many souls endure years of unnecessary pain and suffering.

The spirit of antichrist is one that wants a washed down gospel with no healing or miracles and no evidence of any anointing or supernatural power and its manifestations. He wants to keep the church lukewarm in mediocrity operating in the "normal" instead of the supernatural. He wants a church restricted by reason and logic, that doubts miracles because they do cannot accept what may appear to seem impossible (like someone being raised from the dead, or cancel healed - now when a doctor). They shun divine encounters. 2 Timothy 3:5. But as Romans 8:7 reveals "the carnal mind is enmity against God"

Satan wants us to experiment with witchcraft, the occult, mediums, astrology and other substitutions of power (he wants us to think we are God), while God wants us to submit to him so that God's supernatural power can flow through us.

The sinner and those who have become indoctrinated in the lukewarm gospel that is prevalent today prefer religion rather than witnessing the supernatural power which may expose their sinful nature. **1 Cor. 2:4** says basically that our faith must be founded on God's power alone, not on the doctrines of the church.

Many God fearing ministries that believe in healing and miracles do not get to see any deliverance among their congregation. It is not because they don't deserve healing, it is just that they do not know how or refuse to apply the principles that lead to deliverance. We are not only talking about deliverance from an illness, but deliverance drugs, alcohol, poverty, loneliness, and just about anything that reduces our quality of life.

This same spiritual paralysis trickles down to their congregation. Many believers may pray for years and never realize an answer or solution to their problem. They try real hard to hear the voice of God. But that may indeed be what is hindering them from getting an answer. They are trying too hard which may just be a sign of lack of faith.

God does not show up when mediocrity abounds and his name is merely tolerated. He shows up where his name is celebrated, adored and worshipped. When we boldly and confidently recite Jesus words in the gospels, that authority is confirmed with supernatural evidence from the Holy Spirit.

Many people shy away from healing masses, the laying of hands and all the things that the bible reveals as happening when the Holy Spirit was introduced at Pentecost (Acts 2), because they are afraid of being labeled a "religious fanatic." Well all that this demonstrates is that they are too embarrassed to confess God and Jesus to their fellow man. As Jesus clearly warns in **John 3:36** *"Whoever believes in the Son has eternal life, but whoever **rejects** the Son will not see life, for God's wrath remains on them."* Also **John 12:48**: *"There is a judge for the one who **rejects** me and does not accept my words; the very words I have spoken will condemn them at the last day."*

The True Church

The Christian church is the only representative authorized and enabled to carry out God's supernatural power here on earth. As Revelation teaches (Rev:1-5-6; 5:9-10; Exodus 19:5-6; Psalm 50:5; Deuteronomy 28:13; 1 Peter 2:5; 2:9; Deuteronomy 32:9) we are kings and priests given Christ's authority to receive and administer miracles. As kings and priests we have the authority (from Christ) to demonstrate kingdom power here on earth. We have the authority over all types of afflictions here on earth.

When you believe in the impossible you will see impossibilities bow down before the Lord.

Chapter 5 - Examples of Supernatural Manifestations

Many think that it is impossible for them or anyone outside of Jesus to perform miracles. Well I have more shocking news for you; even Jesus himself was incapable of performing any miracles in his own mortal state without kingdom power from above. In **John 5:19** Jesus says: "the Son can do nothing of Himself".

The things of this earth, such as sickness, pain, suffering, addictions and all other afflictions and problems are no match to the supernatural power of God! Most of us may have never witnessed a miracle, but that does not mean that it is not happening all over the world. For some reason miracles don't make it to the evening news. Wonder why?

The mainstream media would rather cover the evil around us instead of the kingdom of God. It is clear that Satan has a strong grasp on the media as it is powerful tool to influence our minds. Sad but true! This is why it is so important for Gods people to demonstrate God's far superior power to do good, then to allow the media to disrupt our peace by just covering the bad news and the failures of mankind that Satan wants to saturate our mind with.

Satan wants to fill our mind with sorrow, fear and feelings of hopelessness. He wants us to be miserable and sick. God on the other hand, wants to fill our minds with joy, love and peace. Satan controls the media since he is the "prince of the power of the air", but Jesus is the Prince of peace". You can have peace in this side of the cosmos, because greater is he who is in you (the Holy Spirit) than he who is in the world (Satan).

Of course we should not blame it all on the media. Most have never witnessed a miracle because they allow Satan to fill their mind with doubt and their hearts with fear. They are intimidated from ever entering a church that practices healing and holds regular healing meetings.

But it is your choice and you can only take one side. It will be taken either by choice or by your actions. When you take the middle ground you are de facto siding with the prince of darkness.

In this important chapter, we will explore example of miracles and related manifestations

Healing - One of the Manifestations of the Supernatural Power of God

In Mathew 11:4-5 Jesus tells John that the evidence that he is the Messiah was by his healing ministry. The supernatural fruit (healing) that God's kingdom produced was the evidence of his deity. Just as prophesied in **Isaiah 29:18, 35:4-6; 61:1-2**

The real examples below of miracles that happen throughout the land every day are difficult accept or believe if you have a "natural" mindset. When you operate and live in the natural your mind refuses to accept anything that is supernatural. To the "natural thinker" the supernatural is unnatural. But to the person with a renewed mind (and we will discuss how to renew your mind), the supernatural becomes the new normal!

The examples below are just a few miracles that have been witnessed by different ministers and pastors and their congregation from across the country and other parts of the world.

As a youth Chad had a rebellious spirit and got involved in drugs, alcohol and the occult. While in his lost state he started having demonic visions. Then one day he had a vision and he could see Jesus reaching to him weeping. Jesus gave him an ultimatum "be my best friend or be handed over to Satan"! He wisely chose Jesus! As soon as he committed his life to the Lord - the desire for drugs and alcohol instantly left him."

Now years later as a strong Christian and minister he prayed for a man born blind from birth. He was born with no eyeballs. Upon laying hands on this man, they were formed instantly. Now get this - the man's eyes were initially blue and he could not see perfectly. But gradually his eye color changed to brown and he could now see perfectly. Did you know that babies sometimes are born with baby blue eyes and cannot see clearly at first but when their eyes mature to their natural color - they then can see clearly? The point here is that God gave this blind man the perfect brand new eyes that he missing at birth! Yep, brand new eyes - right out of the box! Is God awesome or what!

A woman who could not hear was given new perfect hearing.

In his book "Unlocking Heaven", Kevin Dedman writes of many supernatural experiences he has had while healing others.

A drug addict and an alcoholic were totally healed.

Paulo was addicted to drugs by the age of 16. He was miraculously released from this bondage and became a pastor of a large congregation dedicated to saving souls for the lord.

A pastor scheduled a Christian revival event with thousands of attendees. It would be held at an open stadium with no dome. Unfortunately heavy rain was schedule for the night of the event. Instead of canceling the event he boldly prayed for the rain to stop.

Well the rain did not stop until just before the event started and then the clouds dissipated and gave way to a clear starlit night!

Tony (author) states that "*the Presence and Power of the Lord is here; when you receive a revelation of the word, and you respond to revelation (word of knowledge), then you will release a supernatural manifestation of healing for either yourself or others.*"

Guillermo (pastor and author), has witnessed people being raised from the dead and has trained other ministry members to do the same.

John (Christian minister): claims that the Lord revealed to him that he could have his spiritual senses activated, that he could see into the supernatural. After this revelation, for 2 weeks straight anyone he touched was instantly healed.

A woman suffering from breast cancer had her breast fully healed and restored.

A deaf person was completely healed.

A woman had her eyes restored so that she could see again from her right eye.

A pregnant woman with a dead baby in her womb (her doctor had pronounced it dead), received a kingdom miracle when after a person prayed for her - at her following checkup, the doctor declared the baby alive and healthy.

A person who had died from a terrible bus accident, started breathing again after being prayed over by a bystander who was filled with the spirit.

There are 2 examples of separate families who held activities to feed the hungry. In both cases the supply of food was much less that the amount of hungry mouths that showed up. In both cases they prayed and witnessed that every time they went to the kitchen to get the last batch of food, the pots and food baskets had been miraculously replenished. In one case they were able to feed everyone, while in the other case there were leftovers!

A man was completely healed of life threatening tumors after receiving prayer. He had previously been given 2 weeks to live.

A man, who had been paralyzed from the hip down after a serious fall from a building, had his legs instantly healed upon receiving prayer from a team that was filled with kingdom power.

A woman suffered from excruciating pain because she had no more cartilage left in her knees. Upon prayer she was immediately healed.

A woman who had esophageal cancer felt the fire of God come upon her. She turned to her husband and said, "God healed me." Just to be certain they went to the doctor who had stated "This kind doesn't go away." When he examined her he proclaimed in utter astonishment "Not only is it gone, you have a brand new esophagus!"

A man received a word of knowledge about a person that he had just met. After he confronted her about her thoughts, she confessed that she was contemplating suicide - they prayed together and she was instantly healed of those thoughts.

A lady with a brain tumor the size of a baseball was close to death and could barely hear or speak, when ministry members sang songs of worship, she suddenly proclaimed that she could hear, and speak and that her pain was completely gone. They did not even have to lay hands on her because her faith had healed her.

A woman who was bedridden suffering from Fibromyalgia received prayer and was instantly healed.

A woman with lung cancer claims she was healed and could breath freely again.

At age 39, after many years of missionary service for the Lord, Mike had received a promise from God that he would marry and have a son. Well his wife was soon informed by her doctor that she could not bear children. But they did not lose faith and his wife received a miraculous childbirth (NOTE: Satan always tries to cause doubt and to derail God's promises). When the child was born he was almost still born due to the umbilical cord having been wrapped around his neck - the doctors thought that he would be brain dead. Well the child is perfectly healthy now - with a photographic memory to boot! The seed of the righteous shall be delivered (Psalm).

Kingdom power is not just for healing miracles, but it can be released for just about any need. This includes deliverance from addictions, loneliness, poverty, anger, hatred, insecurity, and anything that reduces our quality of life (Deuteronomy 8:18; Isaiah 48:17).

When a person receives a miracle there is not only healing but an overwhelming sense of peace and love. This is promised throughout the bible (Isaiah 32:17; 57:19-21 Nehemiah 8:10). The glory of God is full of love and peace.

Casting out Demons

Many people are deadly afraid to cast out demons, and they fear that when the demon jumps out of their subject they will jump inside you (just like the horror movies and

Satan want us to believe). We are not to fear the devil, but to fear the Lord. The bible teaches "The fear of the Lord is the beginning of wisdom" **Psalm 111:10**. There is no reason to fear the adversary because he who is inside you (the Holy Spirit) is greater than he who is in the world.

We also read in **Luke 10:19** that we have been empowered with authority over the enemy. When we do it in faith, these demons must flee when we execute our authority in Jesus name. **Mathew 16:18** teaches that the gates of hell will not prevail against us. Also, **Isaiah 54:17** teaches us that "no weapon formed against us will prosper".

When we unlock the supernatural blessings from God we replace the stress, sickness, unhappiness, sin, emptiness and all those earthly burdens with wisdom, health, wholeness, joy, peace, and many more of the heaven on earth well-being that every person aspires to have. It is an abundant life with no limits.

Once delivered from the clutches of mediocrity that the enemy wants us live in, we will experience more joy, peace and well-being that we all aspire to live in.

So what happens when kingdom power is manifested?

- Lives are set free from bondage
- Bodies are healed and restored
- Sadness and depression is lifted from people's minds
- Businesses grow healthy
- Relationships are restored
- Goals are achieved
- Marriages are strengthened
- Families are reunited and blessed
- Churches grow
- God once again becomes the focus in our lives.

Chapter 6 - Overcoming Hurdles that keep us from Receiving Kingdom Power

When our mind is renewed by the Holy Spirit, we begin to see things in god's perspective. We are guided by the inner voice of the spirit of God as he speaks to us in our heart. We are not easily deceived as our senses are heightened so that we can discern more acutely between good and evil. We make the right decisions in our life because earthly knowledge is replaced by Godly wisdom.

Just like the gate and door to your home, the heavenly gates are closed to strangers (the unsaved) and open to those who are part of God's family (the saved). Jesus is the gate to heaven. When we accept him as our Lord and savior it opens the gate of heaven to us since we are now part of the family of God (John 10:9, and Mathew 16:18-19).

Today the church is representative of the gate to heaven (does not necessarily mean a physical church - but our sanctified bodies which allows the Holy Spirit to dwell inside each of us). There also exists a gate of hell where one can slip into if he or she welcomes Satan and his evil thoughts into their mind and life whether intentionally or unintentionally. Again, lack of knowledge can be extremely costly.

So let our minds be the gate of heaven where angels ascend and descend freely on assignment from God. **Mathew 16:19**

There is an invisible battle that is going on all around us for access to our mind - the battle between good and evil. So we need to overwhelm our minds with Godly thoughts and flush out the thoughts of the flesh. We want to replace our old thinking with the character of Jesus which includes righteousness, mercy, kindness, gentleness, compassion, faith, among other things. We need to renew our mind as Paul admonishes to in Romans 12:2.

So what we must first do in order to retrieve supernatural power from God and manifest miracles here on earth, is repent of all unclean thinking and sins and yield to the Holy Spirit. Only then can our mind and body be used by God to manifest his supernatural power here on earth.

If we have a hardened heart then kingdom power will not be released naturally to us. Even the apostles had to overcome their hardened hearts **Mark 8:17.** Even though they were witnessing miracles all around them, it would not be until they received the gift of the Holy Spirit that they would be able to embrace the fullness of heaven. We need to embrace and adapt the thought patterns of the Holy Spirit so that we can receive the kingdom power to administer miracles in our life and the life of others.

John 5:39 teaches us that in order to receive the full power of the word we need to not only read the word, but also live it. When we have the word of knowledge and do not act on it, it just opens the door for the enemy to sow doubt into our mind (Mathew 13:19).

Unlike God Satan cannot create anything he can only imitate what God already created, and he attempts to destroy, corrupt, or usurp everything that God creates. He imitates and then distorts the truth so that it becomes a lie. This is why Satan is labeled the "Father of lies". While God creates good, Satan creates evil, God loves, Satan hates, God heals Satan afflicts us with disease, God creates Satan destroys.

Since our fight is not against mortal man, but against Satan's army of evil spirits and principalities, we must also equip ourselves with the full armor of God. (Ephesians 6:11-17). Please read and memorize **Ephesians 6:11-17**.

Once we have the full armor of God secure in our mind, we are fully equipped to take on any future problem that comes around. We will no longer be gripped with fear and doubt. Instead we will boldly and confidently face that problem and command it away. If you doubt this then you still do not comprehend the fullness of God's promises that are so clearly laid out throughout the scriptures.

The reason the supernatural mysteries of heaven are not revealed to many is because they refuse to believe the word and to search it out. Be inquisitive for God likes those who hunger for his knowledge and seek him out. **Jeremiah 33:3**
we must cry out for that revelation - it does not just appear through casual prayer or mere curiosity. Ephesians 3:20, 1 Corinthians 2:9 2 Peter 1:2-3

Below are 12 power principles to help you activate supernatural kingdom power:

1) Live Guilt Free: Obviously by this I do not mean to sin and feel guiltless! Rather, accept that you are worthy and have a right to receive and administer miracles - starting today. Jesus death at the cross secured that right for us. It was paid in full for you and me at the cross. We just have to reach out and grab it! When you deny the cross you limit all access to kingdom power! The switch is turned off and you are powerless to administer any miracles in your life or the life of others. Forget the past, it no longer matters - it has been wiped clean by the blood of the lamb. Do not dwell on it - that is another ploy of Satan to want us to think we are hopeless sinners unworthy of Gods fullness. Once you start living in accordance with the word, you have no reason to allow feelings of guilt to restrict and hinder your ministry.

2) Be humble yet bold: Understand that living a humble life does not mean that you need to endure pain, trials or submit to a life of mediocrity or lack. Moses was a very meek man with a low self esteem; yet with God's blessing he bravely managed and boldly led 3 million Israelites to their promised land. At the conclusion of his mission these people had been molded into the most powerful fighting machine of their time.

3) Forgive yourself. Forgive yourself because God already forgave you! God knows that we cannot be perfect in our mortal bodies, so do not hinder or delay your ministry by sitting back waiting to be "perfect". This is not going to occur this side of heaven!

4) Forgive Others: Just as important we MUST forgive everyone that has hurt us in the past or present. There is no place in the kingdom of God for un-forgiveness. This one will totally restrict the flow of kingdom power in or through us. Has God forgiven you of all of your sins - yes! Unless you think you are better than God you need to do that right now. Get on your knees and start forgiving. We cannot harbor unforgiveness either towards ourselves or towards others and expect the supernatural to work in our lives.

5) Think Supernaturally. Supernatural thinking releases the kingdom power that God wants you to have. This power nullifies Satan's power to deceive you and to keep you in bondage to sin.

6) Meditate constantly on God's word. Make the word the standard by which you live your life. Take time out every day to read the word even if just for a few minutes. This will format your thinking for that day so that it is aligned with the word of God. Let the word direct your life, actions and way of thinking. We all meditates on something whether we know it or not, but the supernatural thinker meditates on the word of God. You do not need to empty out your mind like those who practice the occult, because your mind is filled with the Holy Spirit of God which provides total peace (Isaiah 26:3). This is how you can activate kingdom power in your life.

7) Become and remain a committed student of the bible. Absorb it, mark it up, take notes, review your notes, memorize them and apply it to everything you do. There is no such thing as being obsessed with the word and the things of God - that is a natural attitude of anyone who is truly a child of the living God. There is no such thing as a "Jesus freak" or being obsessed with the word of God. When it come to the word of God "*it is all good*"!

8) Persevere: When you do not receive an answer to a prayer - stay persistent; persevere. Sometimes God does not answer us, and at times we may need to wait what seems to be an eternity for our answer. Unlike us, God is not restricted to time - he operates outside of time. Many times we do not receive a solution right away perhaps because God is working on someone else who God will use to provide us with the solution. Sometimes we may think we need something but God is not going to fulfill that need because he has something better in store for us at a later time. So we should always wait on the Lord patiently and never doubt Gods promises (Philippians 4:19, Psalm 103:3)

9) Be strong in faith: Accept that everything is possible for him who believes. This is exactly what Jesus promises in Mark 9:23. Kingdom power has no limitations.
By faith alone we have the tools within us to overcome any trial. Once we have fully matured in faith we can command in Jesus name the trial right out of our life - and the measure of faith that we have will determine how quickly the trial or illness dissipates. God does not want his church to have to beg for anything. God wants us to boldly command that storm out of our lives, and the lives of others. Doubt sows the seeds of illness and death whereas faith heals.

10) Keep your body and thoughts holy: Understand that our bodies are a temple of the Lord (Romans 12:1-2), and that God communicates to us through many forms. When we treat our body as Holy then kingdom power can flow through us.

11) Choose your words wisely: Our words are very important, and having been made in the image of God our words are very powerful for the good when used properly. This is why we need to make sure that what we speak is in line with the word of God.
Did you know that God only had to speak the universe into existence, and the universe came to existence (Psalm 33:6)! As His children, God has put power also in our words. The bible teaches that life and death are in the power of our words (proverbs 18:21), and we can take that literally!

12) Love: Of course you have to add agape love to the list above (see chapter 3).

Nothing good comes without a price. It takes effort, boldness and sacrifice to receive the full measure of God's blessings and to release power from heaven. The list above is not exclusive, but it encompasses some very important spiritual principles to apply in your life starting today.

Many God fearing ministries that believe in healing and miracles do not get to see any deliverance among their congregation. It is not because they don't deserve healing, it is just that they do not know how or refuse to apply the principles that lead to deliverance. We are not only talking about deliverance from an illness, but deliverance from drugs, alcohol, poverty, loneliness, and just about anything that reduces our quality of life.

We cannot experience miracles when we operate in fear. Faith and fear are opposites so we cannot experience miracles because fear blocks faith, while faith dispels fear and allows miracles to manifest.

Once delivered from the clutches of mediocrity that the enemy wants us live in, we will experience more joy, peace, health and the well-being that we all aspire to live in.

Chapter 7 - How to Release Kingdom Power

In addition to applying the 12 power principles in chapter 6, in this chapter we will continue with how you can release power from heaven to perform all kinds of miraculous works while here on earth.

It is important to study the bible and know God's word because the Holy Spirit and kingdom power moves through us when what we say aligns with the word of God (the bible).

God wants to reveal to all of us heavenly mysteries. But why do so few experience these revelations? The reason is that most of us can't even accept earthly things so how can we accept heavenly things. In **John 3:12, Jesus spoke: *"I have spoken to you of earthly things and you do not believe; how then will you believe if I speak of heavenly things?"***

As God's children we need to be growing in knowledge constantly and as we seek out to understand the mysteries of God's kingdom then we will receive keys that unlock mysteries for us. So the Christian who is constantly growing spiritually has more and more questions, the more he learns the more new questions that he seeks answers to and the more keys he is given that unlock even more mysteries from heaven.

Jesus promised us that we can do even greater miracles than what he did. Let's read this in John 14:12: *"Very truly I tell you, whoever believes in me will do the works I have been doing, and they will do even greater things than these, because I am going to the Father."*

When Jesus died at the cross, it allowed his anointed (all saved Christians) to release resurrection power from heaven. Without Jesus shed blood for the redemption of sin, there could never have been kingdom power on earth since the gift of the Holy Spirit was the direct result of the Lords victory at the cross. The outpouring of the Holy Spirit is what allows us to continue Christ's work here on earth. It is what allows man to fulfill the great commission Mathew 28:19-20.

You see, power was an integral part of the good news that Jesus came to teach us. Jesus clearly demonstrated supernatural power throughout his 3 year ministry. He taught his disciples and you and me exactly what that power in us is to be used for when he teaches: "And as you go, preach, saying, 'The kingdom of heaven is at hand.' Heal the sick, cleanse the lepers, raise the dead, cast out demons" (Matt. 10: 7– 8).

From the very beginning God wanted man to have heaven on earth. But when Adam fell slave to sin he lost dominion of the earth to Satan - but God would later redeem mankind back to him through the blood of Jesus as he declared early on in Genesis

3:15. As a result you and I now can have that dominion right here on the earth! Satan can watch with hatred and rage but he cannot touch us because we are shielded by the word God, the blood of Jesus, and the Angels that stand guard among his anointed!

Since Satan has no power in the kingdom of heaven, when we have kingdom power in our mind and life - Satan is totally powerless over us. He has no choice but to give up and flee from us because he knows God resides in us, which renders him powerless.

We are all now fully equipped to carry out God's commission upon mankind = to heal the sick, and preach the good news of salvation through the Lamb of God. Those are the instructions that we are mandated to carry out so that we may bless and save as many of the lost sheep before that great day of the Lord (Isaiah 24:5-6).

Our Job is not necessarily to see how we can serve God but rather to allow God to do his work through us. We need God to manifest supernatural power through us, it cannot work the other way. We just need to be willing to allow God to perform his magic through us.

In heaven miracles and healing are natural as everything in heaven is in a perfect state. There are no deformed limbs, or organs in heaven - it all comes down brand new and perfect! Only in earth do we find sickness, suffering, hatred, evil, sin, decay, and death because these things do not and cannot exist in heaven.

The things of this earth, such as the sickness, pain, suffering, addictions and all other afflictions and problems are no match to the supernatural power of God!

We are to not only declare the Kingdom of God, but we are to demonstrate it in the here and now as well, because God operates in the here now.

 Once we let go of traditional thinking and ordinary thinking and replenish our minds with the true words of God, then we are connected to heaven and kingdom power can flow through us so that we can create miracles for ourselves and other.

As priests of the most high, one of our primary duties that we should do regularly is to offer praise and worship to God (Hebrews 13:15). Being our intercessor (Hebrews 7:25), Jesus presents our sacrifices (such as tithes, and praise) to God (Hebrews 7:8).

We Must Learn to Listen to God's Instructions:

A rhema means a revealed word (a revelation) from the Holy Spirit. These revelations of God's word are what keep his kingdom growing here on earth. If no one is witnessing and experiencing deliverance then God's kingdom is not growing here on earth. God is attracted and acts on behalf of his children who desire to advance God's kingdom forward. These are the people who receive revelation that makes the impossible become possible (i.e. people being raised from the dead). Every time God reveals a truth to us, we are then empowered to bring that truth to reality (i.e. provide words of knowledge to a person as God instructs us to) Mathew 16:19.

Revelation is not imparted just to quench curiosity; Jesus made this clear in Mathew 13:10-11 "*The disciples came to him and asked, "Why do you speak to the people in parables?" He replied, "Because the knowledge of the secrets of the kingdom of heaven has been given to you, but not to them."*

We must learn how to listen to the voice of God so that we can receive these revelations and words of knowledge. 1 Corinthians 2:9-10. The revelations that we can receive from God are endless once we learn how to tune into him (Psalm 139:18, Jeremiah 29:11). When you become a servant of the Lord he will reveal all things to you Amos 3:7

Revelation does not just appear through casual prayer or mere curiosity - we must earnestly pursue it (Ephesians 3:20, 1 Corinthians 2:9 2 Peter 1:2-3).

If you receive a revelation from God through the Holy Spirit, you will usually feel a great sense of peace about it and that is how you can know if it is from the Lord, who among his many names is "Prince of Peace" (Isaiah 9:6).

In order to receive revelation from God (through the Holy Spirit), we must have faith. Please understand that we do not gain faith through revelations but rather we receive revelations when we have strong faith.

Once we receive a revelation, we must act on it. If we do not then we are just wasting that revelation. Only when we act on a word of knowledge from heaven can these manifestations of God's power and love be realized. When we do act on it that is when we and all around us can observe a little bit of heaven on earth.

Revelation opens up our knowledge of God, and from that comes the release of power from heaven. That is the power that releases miraculous healing of all kinds of afflictions and gives us direct access to blessings from heaven. We become an instrument of healing and solutions to all those who believe. We are helping God pour out his love through us.

We can know the mysteries of the kingdom of heaven, but the mystery must first be revealed by God through the Holy Spirit, and not some false prophet, psychic or medium. If we search it out we can find it (**Proverbs 25:2**), but we need God's confirmation to ensure that we are not misled **1 Corinthians 2:6-8**.

If we understand and are confident in our identity as priests of God, we can do great exploits. No power of darkness in any realm of creation can stop our fellowship with the Father. There is an open heaven over each one of us, from the newest Christian to the most mature. Being the House of God means we have the exact authority Jesus has at the right hand of the Father. We are entitled and empowered to be His "House," His embodiment on earth. As a Christian at this very moment, you have absolute liberty and access to heaven.

The "Our father" prayer says "on earth as it is in heaven". This infers that when the kingdom of power dominates our life, **we** can do all of the good works and miracles that our Father Jesus and the apostles were able to do. We can even cast out demons (1 John 3:8b).

When our minds are renewed by the Holy Spirit, we will see the Kingdom "see" the Kingdom of heaven on earth. As born again Christians we develop a strong desire to release kingdom power so that we can help others who are sick or afflicted with other issues. We do not just want to watch but also to participate, and to become an instrument of the will and grace of God; and of His kingdom power.

When you are full of kingdom power, you will boldly seek out those in need of a miracle and you will minister to them, pray for them and heal them. You will be tuned into God's revelations so that he can lead you to those in need a supernatural deliverance. That is the level that we all should be striving to get to. To God, that is what normal is. The supernatural is the normal in the kingdom of God.

In the vision that Jacob had, referred to as "Jacob's Ladder in **Genesis 28:10-13; 16-17, 19** - it was revealed that the Lord can allow a ladder or portal from heaven to earth whereby angels can descend and ascend at will and where miracles can abound.
In that story we see how Jacob had rested his head on a rock before he received that revelation. This may infer how when you and I rest on our rock which is the Lord Jesus Christ, how that could open up a portal to heaven whereby we can bring down all sorts of blessings and miracles upon ourselves and upon those around us.

God wants to use us as his priests to allow him to open the gates of heaven for us, allowing angels to ascend and descend on request. God desires to invade this world with his love and he wills that this be done exclusively through his church (you and I); his earthly priests.

As we rapidly approach the end of this age, we need to get serious about serving the lord. We are here to serve the Lord by utilizing one of the supernatural gifts that God has given to each of us. To one person it may be the gift of singing, to another the gift

Of writing, others may have a gift for teaching. These gifts are to be used for the glory of the Lord. The lord requires that we dedicate just one day out of seven to worship Him. It is a day for us to grow spiritually in knowledge of the word, and in our relationship with the creator. This day should also be used to serve the Lord utilizing our specific gift(s) and talents.

1 Corinthians 12:4-11 reveals some of the gifts of the spirit:
"There are different kinds of gifts, but the same Spirit distributes them. There are different kinds of service, but the same Lord. There are different kinds of working, but in all of them and in everyone it is the same God at work.
Now to each one the manifestation of the Spirit is given for the common good. To one there is given through the Spirit a message of wisdom, to another a message of knowledge by means of the same Spirit, to another faith by the same Spirit, to another gifts of healing by that one Spirit, to another miraculous powers, to another prophecy, to another distinguishing between spirits, to another speaking in different kinds of tongues, and to still another the interpretation of tongues. All these are the work of one and the same Spirit, and he distributes them to each one, just as he determines."

Chapter 8 - Conclusion

May the truth of the word of God set you free from the chains that keep you from reaching up to heaven and getting a hold of that power. Once we are sanctified by the blood of Jesus we are no longer sinners, we are now saints. Sure we may sin every now and then because of our inherent sin nature - but we no longer practice sin (willfully engage in ongoing sin). When we accept Christ as our lord and savior we are dead to sin. In other words that sin no longer existed - it is wiped clean. You don't need to allow Satanic guilt to mess with our mind, and make you feel unworthy to serve the Lord (read **Romans 8:38-39**).

The kingdom of God frees mankind from the bondage of addictions, the enslavement to sin, all pain and suffering, grief and depression, self defeating thoughts, poverty and mediocrity. It provides mankind with the opportunity to experience the joy and the peace of heaven on earth.

So stop thinking that you are a hopeless addict, sinner, or hopelessly sick. You are a son of the most high and nothing, except you, can restrict your access to kingdom power. You no longer need to live in regret or dwell on the past. With your new renewed mind you are a new person in Christ, with no limits because God does not limit his blessings or his abundance upon his children. Claim it - it's yours!

When a child confides to their parent about a problem they are facing, that parent will do everything in their power to provide a solution or a cure. How much more will our heavenly father who is perfect in love do for us if we entrust our wellbeing to him? God wants us to overcome all the challenges in our life because it creates our testimony for others who may endure the same trials later on in their life and by sharing our testimony we are a witness to the Glory of God. In the grand scheme of things we are not here to glorify ourselves - we are here to glorify God by our good works.

Of course there will be trials and problems along the way for all of us - but when we place these problems in God's hands it seems that the joy and the peace remain with us even as we deal with life's tribulations. We are refined and purified by fire.

When God allows storms in our life he also allows for us to overcome these storms through faith and prayer. Whenever God's children endure trials, it is only to make us stronger and to shape our character into the person that God wants us to become. Sometimes God will allow a storm into our life to get our attention, and to refocus our mind and our life in the direction that God knows is best for us.

Sometimes we may feel that our prayers or good deeds are ignored by God. While God forgets our sins when we confess them, he does NOT forget our good works. Our good works are stored in heaven along with our prayers, and worship, in a book of remembrance (Acts 10:2-5, Malachi 3:16). God is so perfect in love that he does not remember the sins of his saved children, but only their good works!

When we are young we feel indestructible - like the world is at our beck and call. We feel we can attain immortality through some other channel or means, choosing to take matters into our own hands to direct our own destiny and our success without the help of our creator. Despite the earthly wealth and successes that we acquire, In the end of the road we find ourselves empty, lonely with the same vacuum in our hearts that drove us to run circles throughout our lives only to end up where we started wealthy but poor is spirit, tired helpless, and uncertain of our future and our eternity in the hereafter.

We fail to ponder the things that make for peace. Someday when we are no longer as vibrant and attractive who will be there to love us? When we are lonely, who can we talk to? When we are no longer healthy, who will take care of us? When we are no longer able to walk unassisted - who will carry us? When our eyes grow dim who will guide us to the light. When no one cares about you anymore - who can you call on. And finally when we pass on - who will meet us on the other side? There is only one person who can fill all of our needs past present and future, and whom you can count on throughout your life and the life thereafter. He is none other than the prince of peace.

I believe that in these extraordinary last days, God is imparting an extra dose of the Holy Spirit upon anyone who asks for it because God needs extraordinary people to perform extraordinary miracles in these last days.

The will of God is that we live heaven while here on earth with good health, joy and peace. We are to be God's representatives here on earth allowing heaven to manifest itself here on earth by our good works (Read Romans12:2)! We are to be the light of the world, the salt of the earth (**Mathew 5:14-16**).

God wants us to demonstrate to others that our God is a God of love, our heavenly father that only wants the best for us. He is not this angry, punishing, strict disciplinarian that Satan wants us all to believe! Our heavenly father wants to shell out more love than even our earthly mom and dad can (after all, our parents are e just a small example of the unconditional love of God).

God calls us all to help him save souls. There are millions out there that still need to learn the salvation prayer, God needs many laborers because there are now billions who inhabit the planet and they all need to hear the good news and the message of salvation **John 4:35, Mathew 9:37-38, 2 Peter 3:9.**

In an age where the most popular religions are witchcraft and other occult practices God needs you and I to share the truth with these lost souls.

31

Our bodies are equipped to sense the presence of the Lord and the Holy Spirit, and we can train our senses so that we can become even more sensitive to the presence of the Lord Hebrews 5:14. God can communicate to us through others, the word, emotions, dreams and a host of other methods.

So we want to train our senses so that we can recognize when the Holy Spirit is moving because that is when we can receive revelations and impart healing power and miracles. God does not do anything without a divine purpose, so when he moves we need to act so that we do not waste that anointing.

Through training we will gradually learn how to sense that the spirit of God is working through us. For some it may be a powerful sense of peace or joy, for others their hands may seem to be on fire as Hab. 3:4 indicates. It could be a warm feeling in our heart, or a chill across our body. Sometimes you just feel a desire to help someone who is suffering. We may be moved by somebody's situation, body language, or words that they say. Sometimes we may feel absolutely nothing. The point here is that we need to become sensitive to the voice of God.

Once we can discern the voice of God, then we can begin to live and experience the supernatural.

Do not allow Satan and mortal man to rob you of your true identity. We are children of the most high and that is our identity - let no man or evil entity rob you of that divine position. You can claim kingdom power into your life from your heavenly father whenever you are ready to do so!

Remember that the principalities and powers that set up dominions or "gates" all over the earth will not prevail against us! We are advancing and winning, and Jesus promises that in the end, no gate of hell will stand. Wow! So we must constantly guard our mind and thoughts. The mind is the gatekeeper of the Kingdom of God. It is the place of access, transition, and power. It follows that if we are not steadfast in our fellowship with the Lord that Satan will attempt to attack us through the mind. Evil thoughts can replace heavenly thoughts rather quickly if we do not remain focused on the word.

Let's not just sit back and let Satan continue unabated to influence the world through the media, pornography, addictions, bondage, illness disease and anything that can make us lose faith or distract us from the word of God, and from supernatural deliverance from our afflictions. Those are his tools. Don't share his tools and distractions with others, but rather share the things that make for peace - share the good news of the kingdom of God, which is here on earth for those who want it now. Why wait for it until after we are dead?

In these last days knowledge is expanding exponentially and we see it as computing power seems to double every year, and these man-made gadgets can do things today that seem supernatural to the mortal mind. But this kind of supernatural is nothing compared to the supernatural knowledge and power of God.

As in the parables of leaven (Mark 8:13-21, and Matthew 13:33), we want to make sure that the only leaven (leaven is symbolic of growth) we allow in our minds is kingdom leaven. We want our minds to be constantly growing spiritually in kingdom knowledge, love and faith.

God is equipping men who earnestly seek him out in these last days with supernatural knowledge from heaven. Almighty God, who surpasses all of mankind's intelligence to the infinite degree, just needs the right people who can administer his power here on earth. In the interim we all need to absorb all of the knowledge that the infinite God can impart on our finite minds. (Read Amos 9:13).

All we need is to tune in to this heavenly knowledge and power, and apply the gifts that God has imparted upon each of us to make a change to those whom we come in contact with throughout our life's journey.

Jesus is the sole high priest of God and that is why he is the only way to God (Hebrews 5:6; 7:24-25; 8:6; John 14:6). Through him we can be fully empowered to carry out his mission of healing and saving lives for God's kingdom. Jesus said: *"I am the way and the truth and the life. No one comes to the Father except through me." John 14:6*

Jesus promises eternal life to all who believe in him. In **John 11:25-26** we read: *"I am the resurrection and the life. The one who believes in me will live, even though they die; and whoever lives and believes in me shall never die. Do you believe this?"*

No one else in history has and can make such a bold claim! It is time to take him seriously before this age winds down. And this is coming down very soon. How do we know? Well all prophecies have been already fulfilled except those of the very last days! In **Mathew chapter 24:3-44** Jesus prophesied all of the end time signs - all of which are happening today!

It is truly a privilege and an honor to share this important information with you. I pray that you will not only appreciate the powerful truths revealed herewith, but that you will apply it in your life and share it; that you may become a beacon of light, hope and comfort for all of the afflicted who are blessed by your good works.

And Jesus said: *"I have given you authority to trample on snakes and scorpions and to overcome all the power of the enemy; nothing will harm you."* Luke 10:19

"I will give you the keys of the kingdom of heaven; whatever you bind on earth will be bound in heaven, and whatever you loose on earth will be loosed in heaven." Mathew 16:19

The message of the transference of kingdom power was one of the main messages of Jesus' ministry. It was a major part of the gospels (the Good News), and it grants us great authority. Whatever we bind has already been bound **Mathew 16:19**. Our task is to see what is bound up there, and then bind it down here. Whatever is free in the heavenly realm to function needs to be released here by us. We are to be a gateway for the free flow of heavenly blessings and miracles upon the inhabitants of the earth, so that salvation can span the entire globe.

May God richly bless you and your loved ones in the now and hereafter.

Get Complimentary Access to: "Prophecy Alerts"

Dear Reader: Prophecies are being fulfilled so rapidly in these last days that I am offering my readers complimentary access to "*prophecy alerts*" so that you get "*Breaking Prophecy News*" as soon as it breaks...Just follow this link below and sign Up today...
http://robertritebooks.com/prophecy-alerts/

About Robert Rite

Robert Rite is the author of over 18 books including:

- "Apocalypse Countdown - 2015 to 2021"
- "Apocalypse Codes - Decoding the Prophecies in the Book of Daniel"
- "100 Proofs that the Bible is the Inspired Word of God and Scientifically Accurate"
- "Ancient Apocalypse Codes"
- "Awaken the Supernatural You!"
- "Aliens, Fallen Angels, Nephilim and the Supernatural"
- "Babylon the Great is Fallen, is Fallen! Who is "Mystery Babylon" of the End of Days?"
- "Blood Moons Rising"
- "Be healed!....How to Unlock the Supernatural Healing Power of God"
- "Bible Verses for Supernatural Blessings"
- End of Days
- "God, Mystery Religions, Cults, and the coming Global Religion"
- "Prophecies of the Apocalypse: Unlocking the End Time Prophetic Codes as Revealed by the Ancient Prophets"
- "Revelation Mysteries Decoded: Unlocking the Secrets of the coming Apocalypse"
- "Signs in the Heavens, Divine Secrets of the Zodiac & the Blood Moons of 2014!"
- "The New Age Movement vs. Christianity: and the Coming Global Religion"
- "Unlocking the Supernatural Power of Prayer"
- "128 Powerful Bible Verses that can Save Your Life!"

Robert is also the creator of over 135 articles on bible facts, and end-of-day mysteries and prophecies among other related topics. Visit Robert at RobertRiteBooks.com for sample chapters, press releases and related information.

Says Robert Rite:
"It is said that the truth at times is more stimulating than fiction. So have the best of both worlds, and stimulate your mind and soul with subject matter - that really matters"

Robert Rite - Social Profiles:

Blog URLs:
http://RobertRiteBooks.com

Amazon Author Page: http://www.amazon.com/-/e/B00GOGIBEG

Facebook Page: https://www.facebook.com/robertritebooks

Robert Rite at Twitter
Twitter Handle: @robertrite

You Tube Channel:
https://www.youtube.com/channel/UCbED4FN2Pww-u-o1uO0qylQ

Google Plus URL: https://plus.google.com/u/0/100112453810665259776/posts/p/pub

LinkedIn:
https://www.linkedin.com/profile/preview?locale=en_US&trk=prof-0-sb-preview-primary-button

Pinterest: **http://www.pinterest.com/frontierins/**

Stumble Upon: http://www.stumbleupon.com/stumbler/RobertRite

Instagram: https://instagram.com/robertrite/

www.ingramcontent.com/pod-product-compliance
Lightning Source LLC
Chambersburg PA
CBHW060646030426
42337CB00018B/3479